THE

THE DI

AND THE GREAT PYRAMID A TEMPLE OF INITIATION

First Edition 1914
Reuben Swinburne Clymer

New Edition 2021
Edited by Tarl Warwick

THE DIVINE SPARK

COPYRIGHT AND DISCLAIMER

The first edition of this work is in the public domain having been written prior to 1926. This edition, with its cover art and format, is all rights reserved.

In no way may this text be construed as encouraging or condoning any harmful or illegal act. In no way may this text be construed as able to diagnose, treat, cure, or prevent any disease, injury, symptom, or condition.

THE DIVINE SPARK

FOREWORD

This short text is actually a compilation of two separate essays, the first on the mystical concept of the body of a person being roughly equivalent to a machine- that is, its engine therefore needing air in order for fuel to combust- this "spark" is likened to the actual spark plug in an automobile, and proper breathing exercises commended as highly effective and even necessary in order to achieve good health and, potentially, immortality.

The second entry is by and large a lengthy expose on the Great Pyramid, speaking about its purported usage as a place of initiation (with the Kings' and Queens' chambers and the great Ante-chamber and their usages explicitly focused on) and how the unfinished nature and the overall shape of the pyramid shows its connection to the divine, finishing by exhorting Masonry to adopt similar spiritual principles.

The work alludes several times to the illuminati- it is not entirely clear if the allusion is a reference to the Bavarian illuminati of the 18th century or to some contemporary order using the same name.

This edition of "The Divine Spark" has been carefully edited for format and content. Care has been taken to retain all original intent and meaning.

THE DIVINE SPARK

INTRODUCTORY

The two articles making up this booklet formerly appeared in the monthly magazine, "The Initiates and the People."

The demand for these articles in book form has been so great that it ha,s been considered wise to issue the booklet, to be used as propaganda work. In fact, so great has been the interest in these particular articles that one student, a Mason of high standing, has ordered 1,000 copies of the booklet, which he promises to sell to his fellow Masons.

This, coming at the present time, is to be viewed as an encouraging sign- a time in which the peoples of the nations seem utterly to forget their God and to accept nothing except what eye can see and touch feel, a time in which the nations are torn asunder in the most bloody warfare that has ever been known to man.

Why has this cruel warfare between the nations become necessary? The reason for this is to be traced to the fact that the people of one nation had forgotten their God, had lost sight of the true and living God and had become enamored with the idea of a material god, the god of war, the god of materialism. This people, well meaning and home loving, as time went on, came to accept the philosophy of its savants. And so cleverly had this pagan philosophy been inculcated that its adherents little realized to what limits it would lead and to what extremities of disaster it would tend.

If this destructive philosophy were confined to one country alone, the situation would not be so bad. But as it is, here in America, our large Universities are under the influence of these teachers. Their philosophy is not the philosophy of the ancient

THE DIVINE SPARK

wise men. If it were, all would be well But, sad to say, the prevailing ideas and principles are the outgrowth of pagan philosophy- a philosophy that advocates the necessity of war in order that one nation may become great at the expense of other nations.

It is admitted that the present war has become a necessity. And why?

Because one among the nations, under the influence and power of pagan teachings, accepted the doctrine that if militarism should rule (and they implicitly believed that militarism is the true ruling power), men in great numbers would be necessary Thus it was that during many years of peace the propagation of offspring was encouraged. The impulse was obeyed, with the result that, as years went by, the population became so great that an outlet had become unavoidable.

Not how good and how great the children, but how many, was the cry. Nature became outraged. There had to be an outlet, for Nature always evens things up, as her Law is Balance and Equilibrium.

There are several ways by which Nature may effect the balancing of conditions. One way is through famine; another through pestilence; another still through war.

Her own inherent wisdom directs Nature to use the easiest method. She well knew that the powers ruling on this mundane sphere hungered for war, and that they had, in both thought and deed, been preparing for war. War, then, became the easiest and most natural method by which to reduce the population of the earth, by which to restore balance after a period of stress and strain in the world of human thought and desire.

Terrible as the war is, under the circumstances, it had

become necessary. And when it is over, militarism will be no more. No longer will the cry be for "the god of war and destruction," but for the God of love and peace and advancement through development. No longer will the cry be for more children, but for "better and nobler children," though fewer of them. No longer will men clamor for material power and mere physical prowess, but the cry of the heart will be for life and power on the higher plane of development and service to others.

The philosophy that has exalted the god of materialism and militarism is at last doomed. Men, both in this and in other countries, are awakening. Even in those countries in which religion seemed to have died out, there are evidences of a great and mighty awakening. And there is every reason to believe that the pagan philosophy of materialism and militarism is doomed forever.

This mighty scourge of warfare among the nations is the culmination of certain conditions, the death blow to an age in which negative and destructive philosophies have held sway in men's minds. The ideals and standards of heart and mind have been false and perverted. It is only to be expected that the reaction of perverted principles should be disastrous. Through the mighty force of their own recklessness and turmoil, a bitter crisis is necessitated.

To be sure, the articles reissued in this booklet had in their inception no specific connection with (the war that is raging. Indirectly, however, there's a connection of no trivial import. The war, with its destructive effects, must necessarily lead to an awakening. The wanton destruction of the treasures of the earth, occasioned by the war spirit, has also had the effect of making the cry for this type of literature felt, and thus it is that the war indirectly affects the Great Work which this booklet represents.

When men once come to know that temporal power is not

THE DIVINE SPARK

desirable unless it also confers eternal power, then will they change their mode of life, and this change will affect all the people.

But this awakening will not come until men have been taught, and have come to realize, that they are more than flesh and blood. They must understand that within the house of flesh and Mood there is a mighty Being, potentially powerful, loving, kind, and immortal. They must understand, further, that this potential Son of God does not awaken and come forth by himself, but that he must be awakened by the man of flesh and blood.

And it is this awakening, this mighty philosophy, that the Illuminati would teach, not only to its members, but to people generally. It is for this reason, furthermore, that the article on "The Divine Spark" was written, that there might be an awakening, that man might seek and find "the Way, the Truth, and the Life."

The article, "The Divine Spark," contains fundamental teachings of the Temple of the Illuminati, and that the philosophy of the Illuminati's practical and well received is proved by this other fact, namely, that there is a demand, an ever growing demand, for it.

The other article forming part of this booklet is as important, in its way, as is the first one, and for many reasons.

That the Great Pyramid was a Temple of Initiation is a fact that concerns Masonry. It has been well said, however, that Masonry ha,s lost the key to its own mysteries. The vast majority of its members know nothing but the Ritual, and have not even an idea that beyond the Ritual there is a mighty, a sublime Philosophy, and that in it is contained the very foundation of Religion itself, as well as the basis of all true Science.

But thousands of the craft are beginning to ask, "Why is

THE DIVINE SPARK

Masonry?" And these thousands will not give up until they know.

In this article the author attempts to show not only that Masonry is as old as mankind, but that it has been the guiding hand of the ages past, though then under a different name.

A careful study of this treatise on the Great Pyramid will reveal many sublime truths. Especially should the sincere lover of Masonry be amply rewarded for a careful perusal of these pages. The devout Mason may well be overpowered by the sublimity of the symbology and the ritualistic ceremonies of his craft and creed.

This article contains fundamental teachings of the Fraternity, "Sons of Osiris," an Order not Masonic, but Philosophical, and dating back to the time of Egypt. The Fraternity is philosophical in that it teaches a religious system- not contrary to true Christianity, but individual and mystical- and explains much that would be profitable for all Masons to know.

It is admitted by the most serious of the Masonic students that, if Masons, the majority of them, could be awakened to the sublime philosophy, to the mighty truths contained in its symbolic lessors, Masonry would become one of the most powerful factors for bringing about a higher civilization.

We are informed that "our ancient brethren wrought in both operative and speculative" masonry, "while we work in speculative." But there is no reason why we cannot become operative as well as speculative, as our ancient brethren were. Operative, in the sense of practical freemasons, builders of our spiritual buildings, "that house not made with hands, eternal in the heavens." From the outset we were presented with our working tools and explained their uses, yet how many freemasons of today make use of their working tools, how many care to understand what is meant by "the working tools?"

THE DIVINE SPARK

The Temple of the Illuminati teaches the meaning of the working tools, and how to use them to build your spiritual temple. This is only hinted at in the ma,sonic ritual, and while it reveals, it yet so conceals that the explanation has become "lost." The temple of the Illuminati has the "key" that will unlock the mysteries of freemasonry. We teach you how to become practical freemasons, how to develop the innate, latent powers of the soul, which lead toward real "mastership."

Will Masonry awake? Will Masons accept the truth when it is presented to them?

These are mighty, these are important questions. The author believes that Masons will gradually come to accept and understand the truth embodied in their sublime symbology. He has faith in them and their Fraternity.

May this little booklet do much good; may it be the means of awakening many. This is the one desire of the author. Fraternally,

R. SWINBURNE CLYMER
Beverly Hall, October 14, 1914.

THE DIVINE SPARK

THE DIVINE SPARK

When in normal and perfect condition, a human being is a complete and finely adjusted engine and electric motor for generating power, force, vitality- call it what you will.

An engine require,s several things in order that it may run smoothly and perfectly, and in order that it may generate the maximum amount of power. Two of the most important requirements are the spark and the suction of air.

On examining the engine run by gasoline and the electric coil, we find that that which causes the engine to run is the spark produced by the spark plug in the cylinder of the engine. Here, when the two points come together through the revolution of the wheel, the spark is created; and when the spark is created, or when ignition takes place, the gasoline drawn into the engine is set afire. Thus a force is produced, which causes the engine to run. Every new spark gives new life, and there is a steady motion of the engine, a steady generation of power, which continues as long as there is a spark and as long as there is gasoline to give life to the engine.

There is another important factor in the generation of power, or in the running of an engine. Though this factor is something that is entirely free, yet it is none the less necessary, just as necessary as the spark and the gasoline. For, without it, and even without just the right proportion of it, the engine either will not run at all or, if it does run, will not produce the maximum amount of power.

This important factor is air. At each revolution of the wheels, at each movement of the cylinder, back and forward, a certain amount of air is taken into the cylinder at the same time that gasoline is drawn in or up; and the gasoline mixing with the

THE DIVINE SPARK

air produces gas, which is ignited and which, when set afire by the spark, produces the power. This much concerning the engine, for the reason that the gasoline engine is, in principle, an exact prototype of the human body, and, exactly as power is generated in the engine, so it is generated in the human body.

As already stated, the engine must have air in order that it may produce power. Furthermore, it must have the proper amount of air in order to produce the maximum amount of power. If there is too little air, the engine will not produce the proper amount of power. Or, with an insufficiency of air, it may smoke or manifest other "contrary ways" of a gasoline engine. Other conditions also may interfere with the perfect running of the engine and with the generation of the highest amount of power. The batteries may be weak, so that the current producing the spark is weak. In this case, there will be missing sparks, and the energy is thereby reduced. Again, the spark point may be coated with smoke. In this case also, there will be missing of sparks and reducing of energy. Indeed, the spark plug may be coated to such an extent that it is no longer possible for the contact to produce a spark, and the engine may stop running altogether, or its running may be so unsteady that there is practically no power.

In the human body, we find conditions exactly like those of the engine. And it is for the purpose of better explaining the Divine Spark in man that the engine has been taken as an illustration. In fundamental respects, the analogy between them is perfect. Let it be clearly understood, however, that the illustration is used as an analogy merely, and that analogy is never absolutely exact in all details, Therefore, the reader must not press the corresponding features too far, lest he become bewildered in a maze of questions that might occur to his mind.

The Divine Spark is the name by which Initiates designate the soul in embryo. Few people understand the mystery ,surrounding the soul of man. In fact, it cannot be understood

THE DIVINE SPARK

through mere intellectual comprehension. Growth and development of soul itself is necessary to a satisfactory grasp of the mystery surrounding the Divine Spark. Nevertheless, the analogy existing between conditions on the material plane and those on the spiritual furnishes a reliable basis from which to view the subject. To some minds especially, the analogy existing between the human organism and the engine and electric motor is suggestive and helpful.

It has already been noted that the condition of the spark plug in the cylinder of the engine has much to do with the generation of power. If the spark plug is covered over with soot or smoke or other foreign matter, the action of the machinery is impaired. Creation of the spark is the secret of generating power; consequently, the spark plug, or the instrument by which the spark is created, is a crucial feature in connection with the generation of electric power. Similarly, the condition of the Divine Spark in man is the crucial test of his power. If the soul is covered over with the soot and smoke of ignorance, materialism, and unbelief, there can be no true power.

The engine in itself may be in satisfactory order; yet the one item of dust or smoke or soot clinging to the spark plug may be the one thing that prevents proper generation of power. A similar state of affairs may exist in the human organism. The body may be in good condition, healthy and strong and functioning properly; the vital organs, the muscular system, and the telegraphic network of nerves may be true, each to its particular part in the intricate mechanism of the human frame; the lungs, which correspond to the air-intake of the engine, may be in a normal state; the vital forces, which correspond to the batteries, or the current that gives the spark, may be of full strength- yet, if the Divine Spark, or the soul in process of awakening, is smoldering under a heavy coating of ignorance and carnality, the highest power is impossible. For let it be remembered that only soul power can be classed as the highest power in man.

THE DIVINE SPARK

Now, in this condition, unlike the engine, the human machine keeps on running. So far as material conditions are concerned, it may do good work. Though, to all outward appearances, it may do satisfactory work in propelling human interests, yet this wonderful machine may be producing only a minimum amount of power because it is running on low pressure, running on a force that is purely material or physical. Under these conditions, the great spark which gives the maximum amount of power is missing.

In case the engine misses sparks and does not generate the highest power, we at once proceed to take out the spark plug and clean it, brightening the points- and lo, there is a pure white spark, a spark of fire, which, igniting, produces the desired amount of power.

In like manner, man should examine the igniting point within himself. He should cleanse the Spark of Divinity within his own nature. He should free it of hate, envy, jealousy, malice, and every form of ill-will toward any creature. He should free it of materialism and unbelief. He should polish and brighten it by recognizing himself as a being of Godlike possibilities. As he succeeds in doing this, he sets the Divine Spark free from the smoky and sooty accumulations that have been reducing its power and force.

Further, as in the case of the engine, there is another item of exceedingly great importance in generating the highest amount of power As it is necessary for the engine to receive a sufficient amount of air in order that proper combustion may effect satisfactory results, so is it imperative that man shall take into his organism a sufficiency of vitalizing air. This is the more necessary in proportion as be frees the Divine Spark of the debris that has been clinging to it. For soul power is generated in proportion to the cleansing of the Spark. And, as greater power is generated, a greater amount of vitalizing air is necessary to enable man to make

THE DIVINE SPARK

proper use of the energy at his disposal.

Man has been able to invent, to perfect, and to use, machinery that is patterned in every fundamental point after the human mechanism. Then, how much more does it behoove him to use, in regard to generating power within his own organism, such wisdom as he is compelled to use as a machinist. The electrician learns to note, with exacting care, whether the valves are properly adjusted for admitting a sufficiency of air. So must the student and the practitioner of the Sacred Arts open his eyes to the importance of proper breathing.

The time is past when one is considered a fanatic because he claims that correct breathing has a close connection with salvation of soul. The artificial thinker or the one who wishes an easy path to mastership and attainment may regard the subject lightly; but the one who goes deeply into soul development becomes thoroughly convinced of the absolute necessity of cultivating correct habits in this regard.

Now, more than ever before, man sees before his eyes the time-honored command: "Man, know thyself." And he is beginning at least dimly to comprehend that all creations of human skill, all machinery, whether the engine or the wireless outfit, i,s truly a prototype of himself, and that the force that runs the engine is the same force that is within himself, and that it works in the same manner so far as fundamental principles are concerned. And, just as air, and plenty of it, is necessary to run the engine, so is air, and plenty of it, absolutely necessary to run the human machine perfectly. More than this, air is necessary to the welfare of the Divine Spark and to the generating of soul power. It is impossible for the Divine Spark to manifest the white fire of vital energy and soul force unless it is fed with the ethereal essences extracted from the air.

Through the act of breathing, the human machine obtains

THE DIVINE SPARK

from the air a current of power, which gives to the body, nerves and muscles, the principle of action and reaction. Through this current of power from the air, the human organism receives "the breath of life." But it obtains more than the breath of life. It obtains therewith a certain energy or force, called by Initiates the Aeth; and the greater the knowledge of the Initiate, the greater amount of this vital sub,stance he can take to himself- This subtle quality, called Aeth, derived from the air, gives energy to the Divine Spark. The record says, "God breathed the breath of life into man, and he became a living soul." Thus, it is seen that, through the act of breathing, God accomplishes in man two things- He gives life to the body, and, out of "the little point of Divinity within," He makes a living Soul.

It is a fact- and one held by the Illuminati as an absolute principle- that, if man lives right and breathes right, he takes in with every breath not only more of life to the physical being, but also a subtle quality of Living Fire, which feeds the soul and generates a divine power. The Aeth, the subtle quality of living fire, is indeed a part of the Godhood; and it is this which stimulates and feeds the element of Divinity in man. It is this which raises him above the animal plane and lifts his consciousness to the realm of the gods and angelic forces. It is this which makes him more than man. It is this which gives more vitality and vigor, more energy and force, more conservation of power, and more skill and efficiency in guiding and in making use of the power thus generated.

Every inspiration of air gives to the blood in the lungs more of the electrical power that is necessary to cause the heart to expand. Under normal conditions, if breathing is as it should be, man breathes one time to every four beats of the heart. The mechanic knows that the machine in perfect running order makes about four revolutions to each explosion, or to each ignition of the spark. If the human machine is not in normal condition, if there is disease, if the Divine Spark is clogged with material foreign to its

THE DIVINE SPARK

nature, or if correct habits of breathing have not been established, the intakes of air may be twice as rapid and frequent; and the result is a loss of power.

Another item in connection with breathing is not to be overlooked- that is, the value of exhalation. With every exhalation, a certain amount of dead or waste material is thrown out of the system. Were this waste material allowed to remain in the system, its accumulation would interfere with the normal and regular creation of "the spark of soul power," as well as with the normal and regular creation of "the spark of physical life." This is the very thing that occurs in far too many cases. In many instances, lack of pure, fresh air in the sleeping room accounts for excessive languor and general debility. The necessity of full, deep exhalation cannot be over-estimated.

Correct exhalation of air has much to do with cleansing the thought life. The system may become clogged with the taint of destructive thought and feeling. Through full, deep, steady, slow exhalations, the accumulations of dead and poisonous material are thrown out. Much more effective is the process if the individual understands this principle and if he consciously and voluntarily "breathes out" and "lets go of" the tainted atmosphere of destructive thought and feeling. Through deep, full inhalations, the pure Aethic quality of the air cleanses and vivifies the system, and stimulates noble aspirations and pure, wholesome thought and feeling.

If man comprehends this principle of cleansing and stimulating the thought life through the power of the breath and if he, practices the art of breathing understandingly, with this purpose in mind, in time, the Divine Spark will have become cleansed of the poisonous accumulations which have been surrounding it. Then it will be able to manifest the maximum amount of divine power and energy.

THE DIVINE SPARK

In the engine, we can simply unscrew the spark plug and take it out and cleanse it with the proper cleansing agents, and then return it to its place.

In the human machine, the process of cleansing the Divine Spark is a different proposition. The cleansing agents are love, forgiveness, and other graces of heart, administered in connection with an abundance of vitalizing air. Exhalation and inhalation are both necessary to the act of breathing. Neither one alone constitutes respiration. Each is as important as the other; and the full, complete act of respiration requires the one as much a,s the other. Likewise, in the cleansing of the thought life, letting go of poisonous material is not sufficient. Ridding the system of waste matter must be accompanied by a normal intaking of pure, wholesome material. Breathing in must supplement breathing out. And an abundance of vitalizing air is required by him who aspires to power of soul. Welfare of both body and soul demands an abundance of vitalizing air.

Respiration is not limited to the lungs. The whole system breathes. The air taken in imparts to every structure of the organism a certain motional or functionary activity. This constant and incessant intaking of air imparts a subtle quality, which allows the soul-center to throw out sparks and thereby keep the whole machinery running smoothly and in perfect order.

Here we must note a difference between the material machine and the human organism.

In the engine, we have simply a material structure, a material unit, which, with the proper amount of air and fuel and with the proper current, or creation of electric sparks, will run until it is worn out and then stop short. Or, in case some particular part of the machinery is broken or worn out, it may be replaced with a new piece, made to fit exactly in its place.

THE DIVINE SPARK

In the human machine, there is the power to re-create new parts or new cells as fast as they are worn out. The process of re-creation is simultaneous with, or immediately succeeds, the process of disintegration. Indeed, so remarkable is the process of re-creating worn-out cells and tissues that the highest authorities recognize it as boundless and endless in possibility; and even scientists of materialistic inclinations admit that there is no reason why man should not remake and renew the physical organism indefinitely. Through the infusion of the breath with holy thoughts and passions, man may so energize both body and soul as to make them continually existing. This constant renewing of body and soul constitutes immortality.

The choice is ours. The ideal is ours to choose- whether we will have a physical machine as generator of power which runs satisfactorily for a time and then stops, or whether we will constantly infuse into our organism air that has been vitalized and charged with a force that enables the Divine Spark to manifest itself as an immortal individuality. The choice is ours- whether we will practice the art of a twofold breathing, thus accomplishing a twofold purpose. It is ours, if we will, to breathe in more than mere air which sustains physical life. Simultaneously with the process of normal physical respiration, we may, if we will, breathe in, or extract from the air, a subtle force or essence produced by the thought with which the inbreathed air is charged. This ,subtle quality or essence enables the Divine Spark to attain consciousness as an individualized soul.

There is this difference between the perfect physical being and the perfect soul being. He who is a perfect physical being merely, lives in the material only, and breathes in physical life and strength only. He who lives in the soul also breathes in physical life and strength and may be a perfect physical being; but, in addition, he charges the inbreathed air with (the mighty potency of his thoughts and desires and passions, thereby producing a subtle quality which quickens the element of divinity in his nature into an

THE DIVINE SPARK

immortal being.

The (Student should make careful note of this principle in the very beginning; for, if he does not, if he thinks it unimportant, he will find in good time that it is necessary to retrace his steps and master elementary principles.

The contraction of the brain, which is the creator of mental forces, takes place simultaneously with the inhaling of air. Thus, brain and lungs, or thought and power-creating organs, work in unison. And, as is the depth of respiration, so is the depth of thought. At the same instant that the cortical glands of the brain are inspiring the nerves with vital force and energy, the lungs are imparting to the same fiber their motion. This rhythmical co-operation between brain and lungs, between thought and breath, is of vast significance. Harmony of thought, constructive, wholesome thought in unison with the inhalation of vitalizing air gives to the whole being the maximum amount of power and energy. If the thoughts are destructive or agitated and if the mental state is gloomy while the lungs are being inflated with air, inharmony results, and vitality is thereby depleted.

Right thinking and right breathing are the two essentials of health, perfection, and happiness. Without these two factors, the perfect life is an impossibility.

For this reason, the true schools of Initiation have always insisted on proper breathing and wholesome thinking. The use of Sacred Mantrams in connection with appropriate breathing exercises is based on the principle of co-operation between brain and lungs. The importance of such exercises cannot be over-emphasized.

It is at this very point that students in large numbers fail. They treat the subject lightly, and consider breathing exercises a non-essential, and even unworthy of the attention of one who is

THE DIVINE SPARK

aiming at Initiation, or Soul Development. They have the mistaken notion that abstract thought and mysticism alone are sufficient to build up power of soul. They have yet to learn that true mysticism recognizes the physical as well as the spiritual, that true mysticism is not weak and inane, and one-sided in its methods. The true mystic is alive, alert, and eager to appropriate all that is beneficial to both body and soul. The matter of right breathing and right thinking seems to the student simple and elementary, hence he regards it lightly. The methods that aim at right thinking and right breathing are indeed simple; but in simplicity there is power. A student manifests profound wisdom in trying to perfect himself in the art of right thinking and right breathing. And, when he becomes thoroughly interested in the work, he will find that to establish habits of right thinking and right breathing is not such an easy undertaking after all, but that it demands as much skill and power of execution as any other fine art.

The thought, the mental state, may be changed, modified, by the type and the quality of one's respiration. Every mental state has a respiration answering to it, or corresponding to it. Who does not know the short, quick breath that accompanies an excited state of mind, the suspended breath of fright, and the steady, even inhalation and exhalation of the mind that is calm, peaceful, and happy? By exercising voluntary control over one's respiration, it is possible to make practical use of the law of correspondence existing between states of mind and types of breathing. To induce the habit of calm, even, regular breathing, tends toward the habit of calm, reposeful thinking. To cultivate habits of deep rhythmical breathing, is to cultivate habits of constructive, harmonious thought. The man who breathes deeply and rhythmically is the man who is gradually developing and manifesting the greatest possible amount of true life and power. He who becomes proficient in thought-control and in breath-control is on the road to Initiateship. He who can accompany inhalation and exhalation each by an appropriate thought manifests mystic power.

THE DIVINE SPARK

Whenever you find a human being that is weak, mentally or physically, you are almost sure to find a human being that breathes superficially, one that does not take in enough air to mix with the energy-giving material. Consequently, there is an improper combination, there results a certain amount of energy and life, but there is also a large amount of unused material, which clogs the system and lovers the Divine Spark, reducing the ignition spark.

And usually, possibly without exception, you find that the artificial breather is one who takes in an over-sufficient amount of food. In this we have an exact parallel with what takes place in case of the engine. Through the inexperience of the operator, the engine is given too much gasoline and not enough air. The result is, while at every ignition of the spark there is a certain amount of energy produced, yet there is also, on account of the improper combination, the imperfect ignition, a certain amount of smoke. Not only does the improper ignition fail to produce the full amount of power, but the smoke gradually coats over the ignition point so that in time it is completely covered over, and the spark can be no longer produced, then the engine stops short and there is no power at all.

Now, food is to the body what gasoline is to the engine. And he who does not breathe sufficiently, but takes in an unnecessary amount of food, gradually congests the system. The center of life-giving spark becomes coated over with waste material, and disease and suffering result. Furthermore, the Divine Spark, the soul itself, becomes more and more sluggish, and incapable of manifesting its individuality.

From these comparisons, let us review the most important points- First, in order to reach the highest stage of development, it is necessary for the student to practice deep, full breathing; for this is an essential, the very foundation of all power, both physical and spiritual.

THE DIVINE SPARK

Second, one must learn to free the mind of evil, destructive thoughts, desires, and passions. He must substitute in the place of undesirable mental states Sacred Mantrams, and constructive, holy desires and thoughts.

Third, the student must learn not to take in more food than the system requires in order to form a perfect combustion and give the greatest amount of energy with the least amount of waste. As the electrician or engineer finds it wise to use the best grade of gasoline, so must the aspirant after soul power give attention to his food in regard to quality, and select only the best and the purest. Would we not consider him a foolish man, who, having bought an expensive . automobile, uses a cheap gasoline, mixed with water or other energy-reducing material? We well know that in this way he would reduce the power and the speed of his machine. And yet, this is just what the majority of mankind is doing with the human machinery.

No longer is it. regarded foolish to teach that correct breathing is an essential, the first essential to immortality; for we are learning a few things of importance from the skillful electrician.

THE DIVINE SPARK

THE GREAT PYRAMID

A TEMPLE OF INITIATION

There has always been, among people generally, more or less of a mystery attached to the Great Pyramid of Egypt. This will continue to be, except among the few who have given serious study to the problem.

There are, one might say, two "schools of belief" concerning this wonderful piece of work. One school holds to the belief that the Pyramid was pimply a burial place. The other teaches that it was a place of secret Initiation, that in every detail ft represents a system whence all true Initiation takes its origin.

The fact is, the Great Pyramid was a dual institution. It was a burial place for Initiate-Priests. It was also a Temple of Initiation, the highest form of Initiation ever known to man. More than this, the pyramid was a symbol, a representation, of man.

The Great Pyramid, often called "Cheops," stands directly at the center of the land surface of the entire earth. At one time in the year, the sun shines on the apex of this wonderful structure, and no shadow is cast on either side- It is then bathed in the rays of the sun, and there is neither shadow nor darkness.

Why was the Pyramid built at the center of the earth? Or why built in Egypt?

It is a remarkable fact that Egypt has never been subject to floods or earthquakes, cataclysms or devastations by the elements, such as other lands have known. This consideration alone makes Egypt a suitable spot for the erection of a Temple that was designed to stand through the centuries as a monument of power and wisdom.

THE DIVINE SPARK

    Call to mind the exalted type of civilization and learning which characterized Egypt during the period in which the Temple was erected and in which it was the center of power. This consideration also makes Egyptian soil the spot of all spots the most appropriate for yielding a product that was to endure the tests of time. No one, not even the most extreme materialist, questions Egypt's right to the title often given it, "Egypt, the divine, the land blessed of God and the gods." Who denies Egypt's superiority in wisdom? Much can be said in favor of the keen intellects of modern mathematicians, much can be said in favor of their mathematical instruments and mechanical devices and of dexterity in the use of them; but what has been added to the Laws of Geometry since representatives of Egypt formulated them?

    Egypt was the cradle of material and spiritual arts. Hers was the art of colors. Hers was the art of working in brass. Hers was the art of burial of the dead. What people pretends to claim mastery of the art of embalming as was Egypt master of it? But, in an especial manner, was she master of spiritual arts. Her Initiate-Priests were permitted to come into direct touch with the fountain of Wisdom. They held communion with the angelic hosts. Adepts they were in the science and the art of Hierarchic Invocations. Healers of the afflicted, and teachers of wisdom and spiritual truth were they. They understood the laws of nature, and realized that their land was the spot to be honored with a material token of wisdom, which should stand undisturbed by the elements through the centuries. This material token of wisdom they constructed with such precision and with such solidity that, even though their civilization might fall, the structure itself, as a symbol of their mighty civilization, might endure, faithful witness to the truth embodied in its workmanship.

    A great task, an exalted undertaking, is assigned to him who, by nature and by training, is best fitted for it. For this reason, the divine economy of the universe metes out to Egyptian wisdom and dexterity the honor of perfecting an enduring symbol of man

THE DIVINE SPARK

in his work of redemption- Likewise, the wisdom that "causes all things to work together for good, locates a monumental symbol in the land in which, for reasons physical, climatic, and atmospheric, it is most likely to endure. The brief consideration already given to these two points answer the question as to why Egypt should have been chosen as the land of pyramids.

But there is another, a deeper, reason why the Great Pyramid, the mighty Temple of Initiation, should be located at the center of the earth's land surface, and why its apex should annually mark the sun's direct rays.

In this respect, the Pyramid is a perfect symbol of man when he has reached the state called Illumination of Soul, or Soul Consciousness. After man has passed through a system of training in self-mastery, after he has endured the tests and the ordeals of such a training, and has perfected in his nature the qualities of love and forgiveness, he comes to the point in his experience in which the Sun of Righteousness shines upon his Temple and casts no shadow either to the right or to the left. The soul within man has become the Sun of Righteousness and Perfection. Its rays fall upon the Temple, the purified body, and neither is there shadow nor is there darkness. Man reaches this state only through living the exalted life, and through enduring the tests and the struggles and the experiences necessary to the purification of his nature.

Once more, corresponding to the fact that the Great Pyramid stands at the center of the land surface of the earth, let it be stated briefly, that the physical seat of soul power in man is also situated at the center of his physical frame, thus giving him greater advantage and greater power and greater possibilities.

In this respect again, are the two alike, the body of man and the great pyramid: both are temples; the one a temple of living, throbbing flesh; the other a temple of stone- stone which, however, crystallizes in its form the vital significance of the

THE DIVINE SPARK

temple of flesh. The temple of stone is perfect in its dimensions and in its proportions, perfect in its appointments, and in its every detail, as well as perfect in its mechanical structure. For this reason it withstands the ravages of time. In this point again, it is a fit representation, or symbol, of man. When man shall have attained perfection, or Illumination of Soul, he will possess the qualities and the essences that endure for all time- he will then have attained Immortality and Life Eternal.

But why should the Egyptian temple of Initiation be pyramidal in form? Why not conical? And, if pyramidal, why should it be of four sides rather than of eight or some other number?

In the fact that it is a four-sided structure, it is a perfect representation of man in his four natures. The fourfoldness of man's mechanism was clearly understood by the Egyptian Priest-Initiates.

Man is of body, mind, spirit, and soul. When he so lives as to harmonize these four natures, he becomes the perfect being. The end and the aim, the goal and the reward, placed before him is this- to make his fourfoldness arise into Unity- When he has accomplished this, he has ascended to the deific plane of consciousness. He has become in truth as one of the gods, and his body has become a temple of the living God. As the Great Pyramid was to the Initiate Priest a temple upon which the heavenly sun could shine, without shadow, so is the body of man a temple of flesh in which the Soul, illuminated through the harmonizing of hi,s fourfold being, may shine without a shadow.

The recurrence of the number four in nature's domain is significant, and emphasizes the wisdom symbolized by the Pyramid of four sides. There are the four seasons and the four cardinal points. Nor i,s the fact that four kingdoms hold sway in nature to be overlooked.

THE DIVINE SPARK

These kingdoms are: the mineral, the vegetable, the animal, and the spiritual, or life, kingdoms. The spiritual, or life, kingdom is seldom recognized as a separate kingdom. It is in reality the most important of all because it gives existence to the others and is the means by which they subsist. Likewise, man is often thought of as a threefold being, the spirit, or the life element, not being recognized as a part of his composite nature. But it must be remembered that, when the life element leaves man, the other three natures cannot hold together, but are cast asunder. From many points of view, the Great Pyramid, in its four-square foundation, corresponds to the fourfoldness of nature and of man.

In the Great Pyramid, the four sides were joined into one point at the apex, and thus became a temple enclosure. In its exterior, proportion and equality and symmetry are manifest in every detail; the base being a perfect square; the four sides, triangular in shape, being equal to each other; the triangular faces ascending gradually, terminating and uniting in an apex the same for all. How beautifully this symbolizes the ideal placed before man! The ideal of equalizing and harmonizing body, mind, spirit, and soul, and of erecting by means of their symmetrical development a structure that terminates in Unity! Then is his temple ideal in its symmetry and proportion, and upon its four sides the Sun shines, and there is no shadow.

The door to the Great Pyramid is in the north. Why is this? The sun of the physical world rises in the east, travels by way of the south, and sets in the west. It does not pass by way of the north, for that is the side of nature by which entrance must be effected. For this reason, in all lodges that are governed by exact law, the seat of the Supreme Master is in the East, and all officers pass by way of the south to the west, and thence to the East again.

The north is emblematic of coldness and death. No man seeks death knowingly or purposely. He seeks wisdom and light and warmth. He who entered the Great Egyptian Temple, in the

THE DIVINE SPARK

very act of entering, turned his back upon the north with its coldness, and its darkness, and its ignorance, and faced the south with its warmth and sunshine. Even the physical entrance symbolized the mental attitude that must characterize the neophyte of the Temple. He must turn away from and give up forever those things which lead to death. Immediately upon entering, he turns to the East, seeking wisdom and true understanding, he journeys by way of the south and finds kindness and mellowness of disposition; he travels toward the west where he reaps ripeness of experience; again he seeks the East. This process he repeats, each time giving up more fully those things which lead to death; each time seeking wisdom and truth more eagerly; each time par- taking more deeply of love and generosity of spirit; each time becoming riper and more mellow in graces of heart. Eventually, he becomes master of his own Kingdom, and takes his place as Supreme Hierophant of his own Temple. If his journeys are successful, he will, in the end, have worked out the proper proportions, and will have equalized and perfected the four departments of his being. His consciousness, partaking equally of the four natures that he represents, will ascend into an apex of Unity; and, with the Sun of Righteousness shining in his soul, there will be "no variableness, neither shadow of turning."

Strange as it may seem, through the continued process of Initiation, or Development, when man has rounded out his fourfold being, he has succeeded in doing the seemingly impossible. He has "squared the circle," or made a circle out of the square. His four-square foundation is crowned in Unity. Of this four-in-one circle, there must be a center, symbolized in Masonry by the dot in the circle. The circle represents the perfect man, the symmetrical being, become such through living the exalted life. In time, the dot, the center around which the circle was formed, becomes manifest; and through Illumination, the Sun of the Soul, rises to view, and man has arisen to the plane of the gods.

The Egyptians regarded the earth as a sphere. "They knew

THE DIVINE SPARK

that the radius of a sphere and of a circle must bear certain proportion to its circumference. They therefore constructed the quadrangular pyramid of such a height in proportion to its base that its perpendicular would be the radius of adhere equal to the perimeter of the base."

Thus again, we have an accurate representation of man in his perfected state- According to this analogy, man's four natures are symbolized by the cube! Through the act of harmonizing his four natures, the corners are gradually rounded and smoothed, until he becomes spherical, rather than cubical. As the spherical surf ace supplants the cubical, through purification, his nature becomes transparent; and the dot at the center comes to view. This indicates another view of the rounding out of the square.

In these various particulars and proportions, the builders of the Great Pyramid symbolized, to countless generations which were to come, the perfect man, result of symmetrical development. The Great Pyramid like- wise stands as an enduring monument to the superior wisdom and learning of the Egyptian Priesthood, which understood these sublime mysteries regarding the destiny of men.

Throughout the universe, throughout all nature, in all things that exist, is seen the Law of Hermes: "As above, so below." And, in time to come, as men more and more nearly reach perfection, the laws that rule the visible manifestations of God will be made to correspond to the laws that rule the invisible Hierarchic and Eloimic spheres. The laws of the universe, the laws of nature, the laws of proportion and adaptation in the human organism, man makes use of in all practical inventions and labor-saving devices on the material plane. The Great Pyramid stands as a constant reminder, to those who understand, of the One Mighty Law of the universe, which, in its many ramifications and in its myriad forms, operates on all planes, including the invisible Hierarchic and Eloimic planes, as well as the physical and material

THE DIVINE SPARK

plane.

For this reason, the ancients inscribed over their temple entrances, "Man, know thyself." If man thoroughly understood himself, his own nature and his own possibilities and capabilities, he would understand the universe and everything in it. For man is himself a perfect prototype of the universe, aye, even an image of God. To be sure, this truth is not spoken of poor, carnal human nature, but of man redeemed from his fallen estate. In proportion to his perfection is man a prototype of the universe; in his possibilities of perfection he represents the universe, and may co-operate with the laws of the universe.

The Great Pyramid, as a symbol of perfection, has still other meanings. In particular, it was to the Egyptian Initiate an emblem of eternal life. The Egyptians were in advance of all other nations in their belief in life eternal. Their philosophy and their science had in view one object above all others- the perfecting of man unto life eternal- Training in the Priesthood aimed at bringing the divine spark in man to such a state of dynamic consciousness and activity that death need not be the end of his existence on the earth, but that continued life should be the reward, or the natural and inevitable result, of his earthly pilgrimage. Their art of embalming was for the especial purpose of again drawing the soul to earth into re-embodiment so that it might eventually reach perfection.

`To the Egyptian, death, or the giving up of physical life, was simply a passing on to another plane, where the soul should be judged and receive sentence according to its deeds in the body, and be given another opportunity to return to the earth for the sake of continuing its work of self-purification.

This principle of reincarnation, or re-embodiment, was the basis of the Egyptian custom of embalming the dead. Embalming the dead was not, however, as some think, with the idea that the

THE DIVINE SPARK

particular body embalmed should be reinhabited. It was done merely with the idea that there might thus be a connecting link between the earth and the soul plane. The custom is based on the principle that everything man touches receives a part of his personality. What stronger attracting force could be on the earth than the carefully preserved body? Another misconception is prevalent even among scholars, to the effect that the Egyptians believed that, unless the body was preserved through embalming, the soul could not return to the earth plane. There is no evidence, however, that this belief was entertained by any of the Initiate Priests, though it may possibly have been held by some of the unenlightened people.

The basic reason for the embalming of the body was this; to the Egyptian, Egypt was practically a paradise; therefore he wished to be drawn back to his own country. It was a law well understood by the Egyptian, that, so long as the body of man remains preserved, the soul is held to the place or near the place of its former existence. Every Egyptian of high birth, loving his country, desired to return to that country, and to no other.

Within the Great Pyramid there were three chambers of importance. These were the King's Chamber, the Queen's Chamber, and the Ante Room.

The Chamber of the King answered a double purpose. It was used as a place for the bodies of the Initiate Kings; and it was used for purposes of Initiation.

The Ante Chamber was the actual trial chamber of Initiation. Here is to be found the sacred coffer, or coffin. Here the neophyte passed through the tests and the ordeals required to determine his fitness for entering upon training for Initiateship- At the end of a long probation, he was placed in the sacred coffin, remaining there for a number of days, without food, so that he might become free from impurities, whether of thought, desire, or

THE DIVINE SPARK

substance. Not that it was possible to effect a complete purification during this probationary stage, but the experience served as an impressive symbol of the giving up of everything that is carnal and destructive in its nature, and the taking up of everything that is sublime and perfect. After passing through the tests of the probationary stage, the neophyte was admitted to the path that leads to Initiation. This is symbolized by the beginning of the erection of the temple structure. The final overcoming represents the completion of the Temple, at which, the Great Pyramid, man, has his apex under the direct rays of the Sun.

But why should the Egyptian Pyramid be used for two purposes, burial and Initiation? Why not have two buildings, one for each purpose?

It must not be forgotten that in the Great Pyramid no one could be buried except those who had become Initiates. Also, it must not be forgotten that the Egyptian Priesthood understood the laws of Hierarchic rulership in the universe. They believed in the one true God as ruler over all; yet they associated with Him lesser subordinate powers. These they called Hierarchies, or Eloim.

The Initiate Priests understood and made use of a system of Hierarchic Invocations, which brought them into direct touch with the Hierarchic powers, They could make use of this system of Invocation for any worthy purpose, more especially for the healing of the sick and the afflicted among the people to whom they ministered. Thus, in a sense, the Initiate Priests were co-workers with the Hierarchies, they served as channels or avenues through which Hierarchic power might reach the people. When an Initiate Priest attained proficiency in the art of Invocation, Hierarchic power was at his command; and, as the soul is the agency of command, death of body did not sever his connection with the Hierarchic spheres. His embalmed body, being retained in the Chamber of Kings, served as an attracting power, holding within easy call the soul that had left the body. The soul, having reached

THE DIVINE SPARK

an exalted state of consciousness, retained its Hierarchic powers. In this way, the Chamber of Kings was a sacred spot, powerful by reason of it,s celestial influences.

For this reason, the chamber of burial was most potent as a Sanctum Sanctorum for the neophyte under training. Here, if anywhere, he could gain entrance to the celestial spheres, and make effective use of Hierarchic Invocation. Furthermore, records indicate that, when the neophyte was placed in the sacred coffin in the Ante Room, he soon fell into a deep, trance-like sleep. While in this condition, he received instruction from departed Initiate souls and Hierarchic powers.

In the present day, those who have undertaken definite training in soul development often have a private room which they use as a Sanctum Sanctorum. By the use of Sacred Mantrams and other exercises, accompanied by beautiful symbolic rites, the aspirant may gain access to the Hierarchic powers and influences. In a degree, this is like the Priesthood Initiation. It may be a slower process; but it can be made in every way satisfactory and profitable.

It must not be supposed that Egyptian Priests worshiped the Hierarchic powers. .Nothing can be farther from the truth. They worshiped the one true God. Their devotions, their adoration, their aspirations, their gratitude, were directed to Him as the "One in whom we live and move and have our being." But, in case of special need and special interests, such as healing the sick, or a desire for guidance, direction, and wisdom, in emergencies, they appealed to, and invoked, Hierarchic assistance, much as one may ask for the help of a friend that is in position to render help. And who, for a single moment, considers that to ask the help of a friend destroys worship of the one true God, or makes a polytheist of him who appeals to a friend in time of need.

The Chamber of the Queen was situated below that of the

THE DIVINE SPARK

King. This corresponds to the fact that the child is with its mother before it is with the father, and, for many months, it yet holds to the mother. In the Queen's Chamber no instructions were given concerning the training or the development of ,soul powers, for these instructions are given alone by man. In this chamber, however, instructions were given concerning the Divine Birth, concerning the laws of beauty, love, and purity, as a regenerating power. Here the creative laws were taught, and all that concerns man before he actually enters the Path of Initiation.

The Queen's Chamber, the Chamber of Isis, played an important item in ancient Initiation. From Isis all things come. Therefore, Isis, as the Goddess of Wisdom, Love, and Creation, holds a place in the East, and has often been called "the Queen of the East." She is the "Woman clothed with the Sun." In this respect, she is equal with man; for man, though being the creative power, is nothing without the receptive power, the power to receive and to bring forth. For this reason, the religion of the Egyptians was superior to other religions, in that it recognized one equal with the other, and often put Isis in the place of Osiris, and then again Osiris in the place Of Isis.

The Lotus was the emblem of Isis, typical of all that is pure, all that is spiritual. To the Egyptian, the Lotus was what the Rose is to the Rosicrucian. Like the Rose, the Lotus is emblematic, not of that which creates, but of that which is created. Rather, it is awakened, or unfolded and brought to life, strength, and Illumination, just as the bud of the Rose or the Lotus is unfolded in the rays of the sun.

The legend of Osiris, Isis, and Horus is known to students of mysticism. Osiris, listening to the tempter Typhon, is murdered. Isis goes in search of him. She finds him, but discovers that one part is missing. Nevertheless, she conceives, and brings forth a son, Horus, who sits upon the throne of the father.

THE DIVINE SPARK

In this, read the story of the soul. The soul in the heavens listens to the voice of desire, and leaves its state of bliss and takes on the body. The one part, the godhood state, is lost. Isis, however, which is the soul hid in the body, allows no rest, but constantly urges on and on, until, at last, man, or the mind of man, listens to the urge, and gradually the Son is born, or the Soul awakens; and, when the Soul grows to strength, to manhood, to power, to Illumination, it sits in the place of the Father. The is the story of the Soul.

In the Great Pyramid, there is, besides the King's and the Queen's Chambers, the Subterranean Chamber. This represents man as he usually is, one living the carnal nature.

Man, or the soul of man, came from the pure state. He was Osiris and came down and took on flesh, and is now in the subterranean cave. Here he may remain, possibly never freeing himself from it; but, gradually, if he listens to the Voice, to Isis, within, he will travel upwards until he reaches the Queen's Chamber. There he is instructed in, and accepts, the life of love, of beauty, of goodness As he masters these lessons, he will leave this chamber, gradually working upwards until he reaches the Ante Room. Here he must remain until he has, in measure, freed the flesh from carnality, and has received divine instructions and guidance, when he will be at last permitted to enter the King's Chamber, there to receive final Initiation, which is Illumination of Soul, or Sonship with God.

From this we see that the Egyptians had a purpose in their Great Pyramid- their Hall of Initiation, their sublime Temple, which stands today so that all may see it, not a legend, but a reality.

As the Great Pyramid was to Egypt, so was the Temple of Solomon to the Hebrew race. Though it is but a legend now, yet its meaning, its message, is the same, and its purpose was the same.

THE DIVINE SPARK

It has been said that the Great Pyramid was dedicated to the Sun God. There is no reliable evidence for this belief. Osiris was not the Sun God of the Egyptians, but the symbol of the One God, while Ra was their Sun God. To the Egyptian, the sun was not something to be worshiped, but an emblem of the soul of man, which, if perfect, would take its rise in the East, follow its natural course by way of the south, go to the west, and thence return to the East, only to appear again in the East, and eternally follow its course to greater perfection and continual growth.

The symbolization of the Temple of Solomon, which is held to and honored by the Christian, while he regards with suspicion the temples of Egypt, is of like nature. Solomon is nothing more nor less than a word for the sun. "Sol" is Latin, "Om" is Chaldean, and "On" is Egyptian; each designating the sun.

But as already stated, these are only symbols for the greater Sun, the Soul of man, which, provided the Temple is perfected, will rise in the East, take its course by way of the South, thence to the West, only h rise again and again in the East eternally.

It is of marked significance that the apex of the Great Pyramid was never finished- This is to be accounted for in the fact that, though Egyptian Priests had reached Initiation- that is, Soul Consciousness, or Soul Illumination- there was one thing they had not attained, namely, Immortality of the entire being, true Godhood.

The Pyramid, as it stands, is a symbol of what man had been able to accomplish, what he had been able, up to that (time, to do with himself. The Egyptian Priest knew that the ultimate of man would be entire Immortality. This he had not yet accomplished, though he had been looking forward to it; and the Pyramid was left unfinished as to its ultimate point (apex meaning

THE DIVINE SPARK

ultimate center), until such time as man would be able to finish the work within himself, of which the Pyramid stands as a symbol. Nor is the time yet ripe when this can be done; for man has by no means reached the ultimate.

The reason for this incompleteness is that his philosophy was not complete. The philosophy to which he still looked taught that death is necessary in order to reach the essentials of knowledge. He did not take into consideration that the number of times death is to be met- whether once or a hundred times- is to be determined by the progress man has made, and that it is possible, if he is willing to make the effort, for him to accomplish with the Soul in one lifetime as much as might be accomplished without due effort in a hundred lifetimes.

The Egyptian did not understand that, having met death once, a second time would not be necessary, but that in the second life the ultimate might be reached if he could succeed in banishing the race belief in the necessity of death. It is this race consciousness from which all men must become free in order to reach the Ultimate.

The incomplete state in which the Pyramid was left should not be a disappointment to the student of symbology. Let it be rather a cause of more persistent effort to realize in his own experience the ultimate "apex of Unity" and to find "the ultimate center" within himself. In due season, with the march of progress, will come "the fullness of time," which will make it possible for the coming race to crown the Great Pyramid of Egypt with the apex of completeness. It is for us to do our best toward hastening the day when humankind will have earned the right to add its contribution to the World's Greatest Symbol in Stone.

To the true Mason, the one who has studied his philosophy well, the Pyramid is a symbol of his Initiation in Masonry; to him also Masonry is an exact copy, step by step, of the Pyramid.

THE DIVINE SPARK

Greatest of all, he will remember that "the Word" has long been lost, that he is now using "a substitute," and that his Initiation, though sublime, is incomplete, as is the Great Pyramid.

When man has perfected his philosophy, and has learned to live the life that leads to complete Immortality, or Immortality of the entire being, then is the Great Pyramid to be completed; and when Masonry finds its "Lost Word," then will Masonry be complete.

Let this be a prophecy to the Mason's Craft: when Masonry has found "the Lost Word," then will the Pyramid be completed; when the Pyramid will have been completed, then will man have found Complete Immortality, or Immortality of the whole being, and the Millennium will then have dawned. Can anyone say that this shall not be? If he can, the Sacred Scriptures of all nations are naught but a fable.

May we look to Masonry for help in completing the Great Work, or will it continue to be purely materialistic? Let this be the mission of Masonry- to perfect the Work for which its outer symbology stands- Shall it be so?

THE END

CPSIA information can be obtained
at www.ICGtesting.com
Printed in the USA
BVHW031642051222
653480BV00011B/1289